Olongapo *Soul*

Olongapo Soul

D.A. Billups

Charleston, SC
www.PalmettoPublishing.com

Olongapo Soul

Copyright © 2021 by D.A. Billups

All rights reserved

First Edition

Hardcover ISBN: 978-1-63837-254-7
Paperback ISBN: 978-1-63837-255-4
eBook ISBN: 978-1-63837-256-1

CONTENTS

Little Black Book

It was a given that I would get Pop-Pop's little black Nissan pickup truck when he passed. My grandmother gave me the keys and the title at the funeral reception held at my mother's house two days ago. It had a standard transmission, so Pop-Pop and I were the only ones who could drive it. Grandma told me that he wanted me to have it because of all the fishing adventures we had in it. I was twelve when he taught me to drive a stick shift. I'm thirty-one now, and I still recall it like it was yesterday.

He pulled over on the side of a desolate road and pulled his tackle box and fishing pole from the bed of the truck. "Park the truck behind those trees across the road, Drew. And hurry up. I hear fish calling my name," he said. After I hid the truck, I ran back and found him sliding his gear beneath a chain-link fence, which had a posted "Keep Out/Dept. of Energy" sign. He told me that sign wasn't meant for us. It was to keep normal folks from finding the good fishing holes. We were fishermen extraordinaire.

"Hide, Pop-Pop! I hear a car coming!" He crouched behind a nearby bush, and so did I, waiting for the car to pass. We proceeded over the fence once it was clear. Once we were on the other side, he gave me a wink, and I took off running, shouting over my shoulder, "Hurry up, Pop-Pop! A big old fish is calling me!"

I was glad my grandma could smile when she talked about him. "His eyes would light up, and his smile would grow so wide when he talked about the fish you almost caught, but your line broke. He was like a teenager, bragging about his little brother," she said. I laughed with my grandma.

Then in the next moment, my demeanor changed, and I felt like crap. Pop-Pop had called me less than a month ago to see if I wanted to charter a boat out of Oceanside and do some real fishing. Just getting over the flu, I passed and stayed home. Out of the blue, he died of a stroke a week ago. This morning, my mother told me that my grandparents were planning on going on a Mediterranean cruise later in the summer. Sometimes you lose through no fault of your own. That's just life.

The truck sat in a detached garage next to my grandma's house. I started the truck and let the engine warm up a few minutes. A San Marcos State Aztecs decal was on the passenger window as Pop-Pop was a season ticket holder to the basketball games. I opened the glove compartment and found the usual "proof of insurance" and registration papers. Then I picked up an envelope that contained $20,000. I sat motionless for several seconds.

As soon as I recovered from my astonishment, I pulled out a burner cell phone and a small black notebook from the glovebox. Pop-Pop, what kind of bait have you been using, and what were you fishing for? I wondered. Inside the notebook was a list of dates and colleges. It looked like a Mountain Valley Conference season schedule for the San Marcos State Aztecs, seeing as they were the only school not listed. The dates of certain games had stars next to them.

After powering up the phone, three messages were waiting. The first one said, "Meet at the food court, same time." It came in about six days ago, just after Pop-Pop died. The second message simply read, "What's up, Doc?" Pop-Pop worked as a podiatrist for nearly forty years. He retired two years ago. The last message came in two hours ago. "You OK? Food court."

There was a place I knew that was better than a food court. I texted, "Javier's Tacos. 4:00 p.m" Ten minutes later, the reply read, "OK." It was a small place with a half paved and half dirt parking lot right on the beach. It had wooden picnic tables on the patio. There was a pier that jutted out into the surf that Pop-Pop and I used to fish off. After a morning of fishing, we would have fish tacos at Javier's.

When I arrived at Javier's, there were two very tall young men; the white guy stood about six feet five inches while the younger-looking black guy had to be seven feet. "That's Doc Bower's truck." The white guy approached slowly.

"It's mine now. I'm Drew, his grandson."

The two guys relaxed a bit and smiled. "I'm Steve, and the giant with me is Michael," said the white guy.

It was obvious that they were on the basketball team. Steve looked to be about twenty-two years old. Michael was maybe twenty. I gave Michael twenty bucks and asked him to get three fish taco combos and join us at the picnic table on the patio. He said thank you in a soft African accent and went to place the order. I sat down with Steve and asked him to explain the arrangement they had with my grandfather, after I revealed that he was now deceased. Steve seemed genuinely shocked at the news.

"Man, I can't believe it. I'm very sorry for your family's loss. I want you to know one thing…It was Doc's idea about the point shaving. But he was helping me and Michael. We were close to quitting school. Michael's folks were sick, and mine were about to lose everything. We aren't gangsters or grifters, trying to pimp our rides," Steve said, pointing at his fifteen-year-old Chevy Blazer.

I changed the subject to the team and asked how good were there chances of getting into the national tournament. I wanted to let the kid do the talking so I could size up just what kind of situation my grandfather was mixed up in. Steve said the team was very good and that although he was young, Michael played with the heart of a lion. His nickname was Simba, given to him by the team manager.

After a few minutes, Michael arrived with the food. Before he could sit, Steve told him the news. Michael stood still, then his hands covered his face. He turned and walked to the edge of the parking lot, and his shoulders fell slowly.

"Doc helped treat Michael with his plantar fasciitis then came to the dorm and tutored him in chemistry to keep him eligible to play. He also helped me out when I had a high ankle sprain and talked me into staying in school. My folks can't make payroll for the business and can't get any loans. I had to help somehow, and Doc knew what to do.

"You know something? I'm the only senior on the team, and since I was a freshman, your grandparents had the team over to the house for a home-cooked meal before our first game of every season. All the players and coaches too. Doc had good seats to our games. He bought two season ticket holder seats in the second row every year. I recognize you from some of our games. Your grandmother hardly came to our games, so Doc would bring one of the players' younger brothers or even their moms to the games. Doc meant a lot to us."

I just had a stranger tell me things about my grandparents that I never knew. "OK, tell me about the black book and the money," I said.

Steve looked around before speaking. "Doc had a system that rated the games by the point spread. And he would only risk half of our winnings. If the spread was low and we were favored, then we could go all out for the win. If we were doubledigit favorites, we could still win, but we would allow the other team to stick around, where we would win by single digits.

Doc would bet the other team and take the points. He called it the safe bet."

I ate a taco and took a sip of my drink. "What's the balance of the cash to bet?" I asked.

"Doc has five Gs for Michael and me to split. He only bet on a game that was worth a star. I once tried to convince him to bet a game that I thought we would win. He told me that my ankle was not completely right, and this team had a freshman guard that was superfast. Said I couldn't keep up with him, and it was too risky. He was right. We lost that game, and the kid tore me up."

I noticed pigeons starting to linger, looking for a handout. I threw a couple of chips way out into the dirt. I could give the kids $5,000 and still have $15,000 leftover. Pop-Pop had some side action going on. Sly fox.

"I got $5,000 right now. Take it and we are a done deal. No more gambling," I said.

Steve looked me in the eyes. "That's what we were going to tell the doc. This next game, on Saturday, against Lone Valley State, is a star rated game. We are favored by fourteen points. Doc's system says to bet on Lone Valley. The truth is, we can't lie down anymore. I room with Michael on the road. Earlier this year, we won a game, but he had to let their big guy make shots that normally Michael would have blocked. Late at night, I heard him crying in the bathroom. It's not easy for me either. I can't look my teammates in the eye after missing three straight free throws."

I stood up and counted out $5,000 and laid it on the table. Steve quickly pushed the money back.

"We are going to cover the fourteen points, Drew. Place the bet. All of it."

Michael returned to the table. His reddened eyes told he had been crying. He grabbed a taco and swallowed it in two bites. "You guys sure?" I asked.

Steve nodded. "A scout is going to be at the next game to watch Michael. I won't throw any sloppy passes or miss any free throws. If they try to double-team Michael, I am going hard to the basket." Michael's gloomy face lit up.

"We are going to win this game no doubt. Doubleteam, no doubleteam, I don't care. We are going to blow in their asses, right, Steve?"

Steve laughed. "Yeah, Michael. We are going to blow their asses out."

I shook hands with the boys and said we would meet here for lunch on Sunday, the day after the game. The Nissan could use a road trip to Vegas. I had to admit that I was worried about that game on Saturday and wagering all that cash.

On the drive to Vegas, I heard Pop-Pop's voice. "A big old fish is waiting for you, Drew." When I arrived in Vegas I checked into a midlevel hotel, away from the strip. The Aztecs' game would start around noon on Saturday, and it would be televised on the cable network in my hotel room.

On Saturday morning, I placed the bet and then stopped in a café for a light breakfast. I was very nervous still. When I went up to the sports bet window and slid the envelope across the counter, I told the gentleman that I wanted the Aztecs. He said that he would be happy to put my bet in, but I must let go of the envelope. I wish we took the safer bet, Lone Valley plus the fourteen points. Now if the Aztecs didn't win by fifteen points or more, we lose all the money.

I watched the game alone in my room, sitting on the end of the bed. Michael won the opening tap, and I was yelling for joy. You don't get any points for the tap, but I had a feeling that it was a sign of good luck. Lone Valley double-teamed Michael right from the start. They weren't ready for how quick he was for a tall guy. He went right between the two defenders and slammed the ball through the rim. I jumped up and screamed, "They can't stop us, Pop-Pop!" They tried to rough up Michael at times. He kept cool and passed the ball to Steve. Lone Valley didn't want Michael to have the ball, but they didn't count on Steve hitting the wide-open shots. Still, the Aztecs were not blowing the other team out. It was going to be a tough game.

At halftime, the Aztecs were winning by only seven points. By now, I was pacing the floor in the small hotel room. After the second half began, I almost climbed out on the balcony to jump. Lone Valley hit consecutive three-point shots while the Aztecs threw the ball away. The Aztecs were winning by one point now and for several minutes each team scored every time they got the ball. They were still putting two guys on Michael, and he was getting very frustrated. I began to ask myself, why did I listen to these kids and go against Pop-Pops system?

The Aztecs called a time-out with six minutes left in the game. A commercial came on the television that was directed right at me. A big booming voice asked me, just how do you expect to catch large fish if you didn't own the fishing rod that all extraordinary fishermen used? I felt a calming wave engulf me. "We got this, Pop-Pop!"

When the game commenced again, Michael outran both the guys defending him, then Steve just lobbed the ball high in the air to Michael. The young kid jumped "out of this world" high and caught the ball in one hand and slammed it through the rim in one quick motion. Michael never stopped moving, and the two guys were running out of breath trying to keep up with him. Five minutes left and we needed twelve more points to cover the spread and win the bet. Lone Valley tried to set a pick on Michael and then lob the ball up near the rim. A Lone Valley player jumped up to dunk the ball at the rim but he mistimed his catch and the ball went out of bounds. An Aztec player quickly retrieved the ball and threw it down the court to Steve. He caught the ball in stride, took one dribble and dunked it. He then hung around the baseline and deflected the inbound pass by Lone Valley. Michael was running downcourt to high five Steve and got surprised when the ball flew right into his hands and he quickly slammed it down. Lone Valley missed a three-point shot and when Michael rebounded the they fouled him to stop the clock. The young kid made two free throws. The Aztecs were winning by nine. Lone Valley dribbled up the court quickly and passed the ball inside to their big man. He turned to shoot but Michael quickly blocked it. Steve grabbed the loose ball and was all alone going in for a layup but instead he pulled up at the three-point line and launched a long arcing shot. It went in. Steve yelled at his team to stay on their man and play tight defense. Lone Valley failed to inbound the ball within the five seconds allowed and the Aztecs got the possession back. Thirty seconds were left in the game. Steve inbounded the ball to Michael and three Lone Valley players surrounded him. Steve ran out to the three-point line and Michael passed him the ball. Steve hit another shot and they were winning by fifteen. Lone Valley missed its next shot and fouled Michael again. He hit two free throws and Lone Valley threw up a long shot that missed everything. The game ended. We won the bet.

I was so relieved that I went out shopping for fishing gear, after cashing in the bet ticket. I celebrated Saturday evening in Vegas by buying a ticket to see a tribute band for Jimi Hendrix. I kept track of my expenses for my Vegas trip in the little black notebook—gas to Vegas up and back, hotel for the weekend, and a new travel fishing pole. I easily dropped a thousand bucks, including my meals and the show.

On Sunday morning, I drove back to California and met the boys at Javier's. I handed them an envelope containing $10,000, shook hands, and said goodbye. I never knew it could feel so gratifying to hand over a large sum of money to a couple of college kids. And the best part was I still had nearly thirty grand left to take Mom and Grandma on a Mediterranean cruise. Pop-Pop would say that was a safe bet.

Our cruise departed in August, and the NBA draft was in June. Michael got drafted by Houston in the second round. Steve did not get drafted by any US team, but I heard he got married and moved to Italy to play in the Italian league. Our ship will hit a few Italian ports. I will be sure to look in on Steve. He owes Grandma a few home-cooked meals.

The End

Olongapo Soul

Every sailor worth his salt knows that any story that is regarded to be beyond reproach concerning its authenticity must begin with the preface "This is a real no-shitter." In this case, there are several instances of criminal activity, security breaches, and compromising situations, so the best that can be said is, "This may or may not be a real no-shitter."

August 1985, Olongapo City, Philippines. The fan vibrated noisily in the corner of the cramped room. The rusted metal cage around its spinning blades was bent and dented from being knocked over on the floor too many times to count. Doug Duggett was not about to take time to do anything about the noise because he was on a tight schedule. The fan, blowing on high, brought some relief to the sweltering heat and humidity inside the small studio just outside Subic Bay Naval Base.

"You look lopsided." A heavily accented female voice said, laughing. "You better look in the mirror, Po." Elizabeth "Beth" Pimatel stood on the other side of the small room. She wore a white sleeveless top and a long flower print skirt. Her dark brown Filipino skin contrasted sharply against the brightness of her blouse. The ever-present smile that lit up her very attractive face seemed even wider as she giggled at the sight in front of her.

Duggett had taped two medium size bags of weed to the back of his legs and was trying to pull his pants up. "I'm not lopsided. I just get excited watching you gear up," Duggett fired back.

"Grrrrrrr," Beth began to growl at Duggett, who smiled and rolled his eyes. He knew that when she felt playful, she would act out the scene when Rocky fights Mr. T. He tensed up, still standing with his back to her, because he knew what to expect next. Her small fists started punching him on both sides of his body. "Want some mo', Balboa? I got a whole lotta mo'!" she sneered, imitating Mr. T.'s gravelly voice.

Duggett tried to cover his ribs with his elbows. "Stop hitting me, you little psycho. You're making me lopsided." He laughed.

Duggett was a twenty-six-year old African American sailor stationed on the USS *Gerber*, a small destroyer homeported out of San Diego and on the back end of a six-month Western Pacific (WestPac) cruise. This was *Gerber*'s second port visit to Subic Bay. Two months ago, the ship needed an emergency repair to one of its radars and stayed in Subic Bay for three weeks to get the needed parts and have the shipyard workers do the work.

That was when Duggett met Beth for the first time. She was a go-go dancer at the Boiler Room, one of the many bars in "the jungle." He saw her when she was on stage, dancing to a Dells song, "The Love We Had Stays on My Mind." After some small talk and flirting, she agreed to get him five pounds of marijuana and help him get it aboard his ship—if the price was right. He knew right away that there was something about her. He wouldn't know just what it was until later.

Two months later, the pair was back at it again. Inside Beth's apartment, they finished gearing up and headed for the naval base. They caught a jeepney, one of the many small brightly colored buses that swarm up and down Magsaysay Boulevard, to the main gate of the base then walked the rest of the way to the ship. On this mission, Duggett was only smuggling a small amount of weed, two pounds he bought from Beth. He was the head messcook and had the only set of keys to the dry goods locker.

Beth was a good smuggler and a great decoy on a ship full of dudes who had been at sea for three weeks without seeing a woman. Growing up in East Los Angeles, Duggett always thought he knew what was up as far as running a side hustle. But it wasn't until he met Beth that he realized that he was just "punking" the game by selling to other sailors onboard the ship. The real money was international, getting the weed to Japan. She had a connection named Koji in Yokosuka, who would buy as much weed as Duggett could get. Beth said it was too risky for Duggett to sell nickel bags of weed to his shipmates on the *Gerber*. She had warned Duggett that the first sailor who would get caught with weed would drop a dime on him so fast just to save his own ass. He got hip that the safer route and more profitable option was to get the weed to Japan.

Duggett stashed the marijuana behind a large box of canned beets, then he and Beth left the ship. Duggett had rented a cabana at Baloy Beach, with accommodations much nicer than Beth's cramped apartment, looking to relax and plan his next move. It was there that he would meet the guy who was supplying the twenty pounds.

"Peep game, Po," she said. "Before you meet Romeo, stop at the base exchange and buy him three Tonka toys for his sons. It will mean a lot to him. Your package will not get pinched even a little bit. And while we are there, you can get me something too." She laughed.

Duggett just smiled and put his arm around her. "Let's go to the exchange, baby." He knew that Tonka toys, Seiko watches, and any Japanese stereo equipment were black market items that you could make good money by purchasing them at the base exchange then meeting a local buyer and selling the stuff off the base. Tonka toys were made of the best material and quality manufacturing. In the back of his mind, he wondered if he was being hustled by both Beth and her dealer, Romeo.

Later that day, at Baloy Beach, his question got answered when Romeo showed up with three boys. Duggett handed a box containing a red and yellow bulldozer, a bright green dump truck, and a red and white ambulance to Romeo. Romeo looked inside the box and smiled. He called the boys over to him.

They were twins, about seven or eight years old, and a younger brother, who looked about five. The kids went nuts for the toys, thanking Romeo and then scampering to play in the sand.

Dory, Romeo's sister and Beth's best friend, also came to enjoy the beach. She had long black hair and was gorgeous. She had been recruited by Beth to help get twenty pounds of weed aboard the navy ship. Dory looked so ravishing that once the trio got to the ship, all she would have to do was stand there and smile, and Duggett could probably bring aboard a hundred pounds of weed in a wheelbarrow and no one would notice him.

Romeo handed over a small canvas gym bag with the weed inside, bagged up in plastic. "If any cops stop you with this, tell them it is mine, and give them one hundred dollars. Just don't argue or make trouble. They will keep the weed, but they will let you go," he told Duggett.

Duggett nodded and handed Romeo a beer and the cash. "We got *pancit*, lumpia, and a bunch of stuff Beth picked up, and I don't know what it is. Let's eat," Doug told Romeo and Dory.

Romeo was the drummer in a country and western band with Dory as the lead singer. They played at the biggest shit kicker bar in Olongapo, Gary's Place, and sometimes went to play at a club in Angeles, outside Clark Air Force Base. The live bands in Olongapo were amazing. They sounded just like the original band in all styles of music—rock, country and western, or soul. When he was not performing, Romeo said he lived on a farm with his wife and sons and that he raised goats and grew real good weed. He was a slim, friendly guy with a goatee.

Duggett was thankful that Beth pulled his coat about the toys, getting him on the good side of her weed connection. After slamming down a delicious Filipino meal, Duggett stepped outside to sit in a papasan chair out on the deck. He looked out at the Pacific Ocean, the mountains, and the lush jungle and really started to appreciate how beautiful it is in the Philippines. He felt sorry for the sailors who only saw the seedy side of Olongapo on Magsaysay Boulevard. Duggett watched the small boys playing in the sand with the Tonka trucks. Beth and Dory were walking and talking in the surf nearby. Dory was admiring the new earrings Beth got at the base exchange.

Listening to the waves and the kids laughing, he wondered what life would be like if he stayed here instead of going back to Los Angeles. He loved Los Angeles, but the world was quickly changing in his hometown. The crack epidemic, and the violence that it inflamed, was not the only thing that could end your life. Duggett remembered back when he was fifteen years old in Southern California on a warm summer day, the Dodgers had beaten the Giants that afternoon, and he proudly wore his blue LA Tshirt to the nearby park. A block before getting to the park, a police cruiser pulled up on him, and a big white cop grabbed him and pushed him into the back seat. The cop got back in the driver's seat and drove off.

"Hey, man, I didn't do anything! Why are you fucking with me!" Duggett yelled, smashing his hand against the metal mesh grating that separated the front and back seat.

"Where's the dope house, asshole? Tell me where it is and I will let you go," the cop hollered.

Duggett got so angry he started to stutter. "M-man, are you crazy?"

The cop half turned to face Duggett. "I know the gangbangers are using kids to run dope for them, and you all wear blue Dodger shirts. So just shut up and tell me where the dope house is. If you don't tell me, I'm gonna drive you to Watts and put you out. That's the other guys' turf. They won't be happy seeing your skinny ass wearing a blue shirt in their neighborhood."

Being a black teenager in Los Angeles during the eighties was a precarious existence. To survive, you better know the tribal laws. In some territories, you wore red or any color, except blue. The drugs, the gangs, and the damn LAPD were hazardous to your health as a black male. Duggett knew it was a possible death sentence to go to Watts, and even in the best scenario, there would be a serious ass kicking in store for him.

"L-look," he stuttered, "I don't know about dope houses or gangs. I wear Dodger gear because I like the Dodgers. They won today 7 to 3. Fernando Valenzuela pitched today. Y-you g-got me wrong, m-man."

The cop drove three more blocks and then pulled the cruiser to the curb. He got out and opened the back door. He believed Duggett was telling the truth. "Get out of the damn car. I just pulled over in the beginning of those guys' territory. You should haul your narrow ass back to your side of town quickly." Duggett got out of the car, and that was exactly what Duggett did.

Romeo stepped out on the patio and handed Duggett a San Miguel beer. "You ever think about a transfer here in P I? We can do business together. You know about selling weed. I can teach you about raising goats. My sister told me to come meet you because Beth likes you. I had to check you out. If you are a *punyeta*—that means asshole—I sell weed to you then call police, they arrest you, you give them one hundred dollars, they let you go but they will keep the weed, then they call me to sell it back to me very cheap. Beth says you are not *punyeta*, and I agree with her. So now I can talk to you about how we do business. Beth introduced me to Koji about five years ago. I have a pilot at the air force base who takes weed to Japan, but he will retire soon."

Duggett learned from talking with Romeo that the Japanese guy, Koji, who owned a jazz club in Yokosuka, was an old flame of Beth. He liked having a good supply of weed on hand to impress his customers, especially the Yakuza dudes. On Duggett's first trip to Olongapo, Beth had given Duggett the address of the club in Yokosuka so he could sell Koji the five pounds of weed he smuggled onto the *Gerber*. For every two hundred bucks Duggett spent in Olongapo, he made one thousand in Yokosuka.

"I'm always looking for good partners. You think about it," Romeo told Duggett.

Beth and Dory had just walked up from the beach and caught the back half of Romeo's offer. "Duggett's ship will return to San Diego in two months. He will make his money in Japan, and then he returns to the world. We won't see him again," Beth said.

Duggett was not surprised that Beth had discovered when the *Gerber* was scheduled to return to the States. He was a little surprised that she was so emotionally invested. He knew she was a hustler and that she got hit on by service guys every night she worked. He was smart enough to never ask her questions about her personal life because he never wanted to hear the ugly truth or the pretty lies.

Duggett rolled up his pants to walk into the surf to reflect and gather his thoughts. He was thankful to be able to see a poor by US standards but beautiful country like the Philippine Islands. Sitting on the beach and gazing at the Pacific Ocean, Duggett's tranquil moment was violently interrupted by the yelling and screaming boys raining down punches on his back.

"Want some mo', Balboa! Want some mo'!"

He looked over at Beth and Dory, who were laughing it up and pointing at him. He knew instantly who coached the boys' sneak attack. Romeo ran over to grab his kids. "Stop beating up my partner, boys." After some small talk and hugs, Romeo, Dory, and the boys loaded themselves into a Toyota van. It was the van the band used to go to their gigs. "Come listen to us play after you do your thing tomorrow," Romeo told Duggett before he drove the van onto the road.

The boys stuck their heads out of the window and bid farewell. "Bye, Aunt Beth and Uncle Duggett! Thank you for Tonkas!" they yelled.

Later in the evening, Beth and Duggett fell asleep in a large hammock on the beach, enjoying the ocean breeze and hearing the waves slide on the shore. Once during the night, Duggett opened his eyes and kissed Beth's forehead. Her face was buried in his chest, so he could not see that her eyes were also open. "L-love you, baby," he stuttered. She closed her eyes and stayed silent, listening to his rapid heartbeat.

The next morning, they ate a quick breakfast and caught a jeepney back to Beth's apartment to wait for Dory. The three of them would tape the weed to their bodies and go aboard the *Gerber* to watch the movie. At the end of the workday and after the final meal had been served, a reel to reel film projector would be set up on the messdeck for the duty section guys to watch a flick. Tonight, the movie would be an *Indiana Jones* flick. That would work perfectly because it was going to be dark, loud, and exciting.

Aboard the ship, Duggett and the girls sat in the back, removing the weed from their bodies and from the girls' large purses. As soon as Dory got her weed removed and shoved inside a garbage bag, she handed it to Duggett and walked to the front of the messdeck. Duggett slipped a twenty to the projectionist and told him to pause the movie, slide the film to the side, and light Dory up with the film projector light.

Dory began an a cappella song by Crystal Gayle, "Don't It Make My Brown Eyes Blue," and it was like heaven just turned on the radio. Her voice sounded beautiful, and she looked like an angel in the spotlight. The sailors' eyes were glued to her as Duggett gathered his weed and stuffed it into a large plastic bag. The sailors gave her a standing ovation when she finished and returned to sit next to Beth. The sailor running the projector resumed the *Indiana Jones* movie. Once Duggett stashed the weed in his hiding place, they all left before the movie ended.

Magsaysay Boulevard led out to the main gate which was manned by the US marines. Right after you passed through the main gate, there was a bridge that crossed over a sewage canal. It was Olongapo River, but it was just a sewage canal. You could smell it before you reached it. It was aptly nicknamed shit river. Kids would beg for change at the end of the bridge. They would also stand in canoes in the canal holding nets to catch coins thrown from the bridge. Young girls in canoes would wear beautiful princess dresses with fairy-type wings in the middle of the filthy canal. It was a sight to be seen. Duggett always carried a couple of bucks in quarters when he crossed the bridge.

Magsaysay Boulevard ended at the main drag of Olongapo City. The white dudes would turn right and go down shit kicker row. That was where all the country-and-western music was played. Most of the rock and roll clubs were down there as well. If you turn left at the main road, you begin to enter the "jungle," the part of town where the soul brothers hung out. The bars played R & B, jazz, blues, and some classic rock. During the Vietnam War era, you would not want to be in the wrong bar, or you would be reminded, in a less than cordial manner, where the door was, and your head would be used to open it. Things had chilled out, to some degree, in the eighties. The military had become more inclusive for minorities, although the navy did drag its feet compared with the other branches.

All in all, in Olongapo, there were too many vices available to be worried about the stupid, hateful stuff. The Philippines was an amazing place. Live bands in the bars sounded just like the original artist. The countryside was rich with lush forests and jungles. Beautiful beaches with white sand were plentiful. The big cities were bustling and modern. But it was mostly the people that made an impression on Duggett. They were friendly, funny, hardworking, engaging folks. Of course, outside any US military base, you will find your share of grifters and hustlers, but even they were entertaining. It was a mainly Christian country, and the English language was widely spoken. The Philippine Islands had a long, hard struggle for independence, and the people were resilient. When you get right down to it, for Duggett, the place had a whole lot of soul.

Duggett and the two girls hit the main drag and took a right, heading down shitkicker row to Gary's Place. Romeo and the band were there setting up their equipment. Duggett peeled off two hundred dollars and handed it to Dory, thanking her for her help.

"Stay for our show, Duggett," she said.

He nodded and led Beth to a small table to order drinks. After paying for two beers, Duggett handed Beth two crisp hundred-dollar bills. "One more, Po," she said. "You have to pay for my heart."

Duggett handed her five twenties. "That's it, babe. I'm ass out for cash," he said.

"It's OK. You got me," she told him.

The band broke out in a Steppenwolf hit, "Magic Carpet Ride" and it was fantastic. Doug and Beth danced on the crowded dance floor and he could see that she was having a great time and drinking like a sailor.

"Hoo-hoo! Party over hee-aw!" Doug heard that familiar southern drawl and knew Tex was nearby. Tex Hearder was a tall country boy from some small dusty town in Texas and the only white guy on the ship that he would sell weed to. Tex wore jeans, cowboy boots, and a red and white checkered shirt to go with his ever-present smile. He strode over to Doug and put his arm around his shoulder. "What's going on, bro-ham? Let's talk some business."

Tex was cool. He didn't have a big mouth and Doug usually let him sell a few ounces to his buddies. Beth gave Doug a joint so the two sailors could go outside and smoke and said she would join some of her girlfriends at a larger round table near the back door. Doug and Tex walked about fifty yards down an alley so they could toke and joke away from the crowd. They were just about finished smoking when Doug spotted two Filipino cops sneaking up, pressed against the wall of the alley and crouching behind the boxes and crates stacked on both sides. "Hey Tex," Doug whispered. "Yeah, I see them," Tex replied. Both men knew the cops would let them go after taking all their cash from them. "On the count of three," Tex said. "One, two."

And Doug took off. "THREE," yelled Doug. Tex threw a few crates into the center of the alley and took off running after Doug. It was quite a commotion with cops shouting and people running around trying to catch the chickens that were sleeping inside the crates that Tex had just tossed. Doug and Tex ran back inside the club and dove beneath the table where Beth and four of her friends were sitting. The table had a large red table cloth that reached the floor. Moments later the two cops appeared, looking over the crowd. A small brown hand extended beneath the table, palm up. Tex stared at the hand and didn't move. The woman who owned the small hand called out to the cops. Tex quickly placed a twenty-dollar bill in her palm. The two cops heard her and approached the table where Doug and Tex were hiding. "Are you looking for the tall white man and the short black man?' she asked the cops, keeping her hand beneath the table. She stretched out her right leg beneath the table and hooked her foot around the rednecks' red neck and reeled him in closer to her. She grabbed Tex by the back of his head and pulled his face into her crotch. He tried to resist but Doug gave him a shove also. "They ran out the other door," she said. The cops nodded and left. Doug and Tex crawled out from under the table and the girls erupted with laughter. "Man, that was close. I got to go wash my face off. I smell like *pancit*," Tex joked. "You smell like first division too. I think she did a division party for them," Doug teased. Beth grabbed Doug's hand and led him back to their small table.

"Let me tell you something, Po". Her words were slurred from all the alcohol she had drank. Duggett smiled at her. He thought she was adorable when she was tipsy.

"Let me pull your coat, Po. If you re-enlist, you can be stationed here and we can be together. I ain't no broke bitch. I have a farm too. Me and Dory have a hog farm that is in the hills. We don't run it. We have workers there. I can take you to Boracay and to White Beach. It's so beautiful. The Philippine has over 7,000 islands and the most beautiful beaches. We can find our own island and be happy there. But you don't have to be the navy's bitch. Every two weeks you get your welfare check. We can buy our own club. You can work with Romeo. He likes you. He told me to never waste his time with a scared motherfucker. He asked me if your heart pumped pussy juice. I said "not my Duggett". Will you stay?"

Grabbing her hand and squeezing it gently, he replied "We'll see baby". She quickly snatched her hand away and reached into her purse. Her hand emerged holding her balisong, commonly known as a butterfly knife. It's a folding pocketknife with two folding handles that conceal the blade, but when unfolded it was a rapidly spinning blur in the hands of an expert. Beth was an expert. It was already spinning around her hand and wrist as if it was alive. She stood up and walked towards him. She danced slowly to the music while performing a wrist pass with the knife. Then she did the basic twirl which was similar to spinning a baton around your fingers. She did an eight-ball ladder combo then flipped the knife behind her neck into her other hand. Her fist pounded the butt end of the knife into his chest, safely pointing the tip of the blade away from him. The knife had a cutting edge on one side, the other being dull. Her little finger balanced the dull side of the blade and made the knife spin like a fan. She did a movement called behind the eight ball then flipped the knife to her other hand. In one smooth motion, she caught the knife and brought it down on his crotch, this time tip first. She stopped a half inch from his groin and slowly turned to him and smiled.

"I could keep going," she sneered. Doug didn't flinch.

"Who is that gonna punish? Me or you?" he asked. She laughed loudly and put her knife away. She sat on his lap. She rested her head on his and sighed.

Romeo and Dory's band sounded outstanding, even if they were playing country music, which Duggett knew very little of. Dory did a perfect rendition of Dolly Parton's "I Will Always Love You," and she came and grabbed Duggett and led him to dance with Beth. They danced and drank until the curfew came near. Olongapo was still under martial law. Duggett and Beth left Gary's Place and spent the night in her apartment making love that was reminiscent to the "Thrilla in Manila". It was fast, violent, and rough just like the epic fight between Muhammed Ali and Joe Frazier. Duggett's emotions were on that ride at Disneyland called the Matterhorn, up and down, twisting and turning, wondering how something that looks so grand can make you feel so torn up inside. And Beth would not back down one inch from his punishing passion. "Go ahead and do it harder. Just like the Navy does it to you too. I'm not the only whore here," she told him. He ravished her in several positions while she taunted him, bit him, kissed him, and when he paused to shift positions, she pushed him over and climbed onto him, and defiantly showed him that she was still in charge. Straddling him and with both hands squeezing his throat, Beth took all he had to give and all he hoped to have. They came together and she collapsed on Duggetts' sweating body. Physically and emotionally drained, he pushed her over on her back and laid next to her small frame and they quietly caught their breath. "Want some mo',Po? I gotta a whole lotta mo'," she whispered to him. He kissed her deep and forgot why he was so angry but he knew it wasn't because of her. It was his situation that had him by the balls.

The next day was Duggett's duty day, so he could not leave the ship. He had to prepare the day's meals and load supplies into his storeroom because the following day, the *Gerber* would pull up the anchor and head out to sea. After three weeks of performing naval exercises with other ships off the coast of Korea, the *Gerber* dropped anchor in Yokosuka, Japan. A week in Japan gave Duggett plenty of time to make his delivery to Koji. He met Koji at the club and gave him a duffel bag full of weed. He noticed a heavily tattooed guy sitting at the bar was missing his pinky finger. Koji handed him a small satchel with cash inside and whispered, "Don't stare. Don't ask. Go now."

The *Gerber* left Japan and rejoined the nine-ship battle group that began the WestPac cruise six months ago. All the ships were headed back to the States. Three weeks of doing war games and drills in the Pacific, a stop for fuel and supplies in Pearl Harbor, then back to San Diego.

Duggett was anxious to get back to the United States, just like every sailor onboard the *Gerber*. Nearly every evening, after the final meal was over and all the cleanup was finished, Duggett would go sit on the fantail and look up at the stars. Words can't describe the serenity a person feels when they are enveloped in total darkness, save the light of the stars above. The rhythmic slapping of the propellor blades against the ocean was loud but calming. It was like he was alone in his own universe when he slipped on the headphones to his Sony Walkman and the Dells started to sing "The Love We Had Stays on My Mind." He wondered if Beth could see the same stars.

Once Duggett reached San Diego, he worked for two and a half months and got his honorable discharge from the navy. He went to his old neighborhood in Los Angeles and saw the devastation that crack had unleased on the community. Duggett had a lot of money to invest, and he had plenty of offers to become a distributor in the crack trade, but he declined all of them because he didn't like the violence that was a big part of the business.

He ran into Trigger, a guy who was a few years older and, in his day, was a major baller. He sold kilos of coke to most of the West side. He must have started to get high on his own supply. He did not seem as solid as he once was. Duggett bought Trigger's Seville for next to nothing. He also saw a dude named Alonzo Tymes. The guy used to be a Golden Gloves champ. Now dope dealers bet on his fights with other crackheads and bums in local backyard rings. The word is that he could still throw those hands even if he was a dope fiend. The dude walked around with a backpack. Inside the backpack was a pair of boxing gloves. He was always ready to throw down with anyone as a means to get food to eat or drugs to get high. Duggett always liked Tymes and thought that he might even become a pro fighter.

On a Sunday, the Lakers had an afternoon game in Inglewood at the Forum. Duggett bought a couple of tickets and took Tymes to watch the game. Going to the Fabulous Forum to watch the Lakers was more than a basketball game. Magic and Kareem, along with the showtime team, dazzled you on the court, but the crowd action was just as entertaining, watching music and movie stars pretending to be normal folk, wearing a plain white T-shirt and blue jeans with five hundred grand worth of jewelry.

"You need to get off the shit, bro," he told him. "You got a shot at something. You can be someone. For real." Tymes just nodded his head. After the game, they went to the car parked in the lot and discovered two cops sitting on the hood. Duggett was pissed but did not show it. "You guys looking for someone?" he asked. One cop was white, and the other was black.

"This is Trigger's car," said the black cop, not bothering to stand up.

"I bought it from him. It's my car," Duggett said.

The white cop recognized Tymes and started to mock him. "Hey, look. It's Punchy. Where's your backpack? I feel like going a couple of rounds." He laughed.

The black cop pointed at Tymes while speaking to Duggett. "Do you and 'Ghetto Fabulous' work for Trigger?" he asked.

"You guys making deliveries at the game now?" the white cop added.

"We don't work for nobody. I bought the car from a dude I know. That's all it is," Duggett explained.

The two cops both stood up and stood next to Duggett. "Trigger owes us some money. If we find out that you work for Trigger, that means you owe us too," the black cop said.

The white cop looked closely at the Seville and then at Duggett. "How many unemployment checks did you have to give Trigger for this car? Trigger always kept a clean ride, for his 'beee-ches." The cops laughed.

"I paid cash for the car. How much cash do I need to get you two hemorrhoids off my ass?" Duggett griped.

The black cop dropped Duggett with a hard punch to his ribs. He stood over Duggett, preparing to beat him further, but Tymes rushed in and slammed his body against the cops' shoulder, causing him to stumble and almost lose his balance. Both cops began raining punches against the smaller man, but Tymes just covered up and weaved his body, trying to catch glancing blows on his shoulders and arms. He did not punch back. Duggett jumped to his feet and pleaded with the cops.

"What the hell do you want?" he yelled.

The cops stopped hitting Tymes and calmed down enough to catch their breath. "Tell Trigger that he better find us before we find him," said the black cop.

"Enjoy your evening," said the other officer.

The cops got into their cruiser and drove off. Duggett and Tymes got in the Seville, and Duggett asked Tymes if he was OK.

"They hit like old ladies with arthritis up their asses." He laughed.

Duggett laughed and started the car. "Meet me downtown tomorrow at noon. At the gym you used to work out in. I got a friend who might take you on as a fighter if you can stay clean. There will be money in it for you, no matter what. Cool?" Duggett looked at Tymes, waiting for an answer.

"Kool & the Gang, brother," he replied.

The next day at noon, Duggett introduced Tymes to a guy he knew from the navy, Jimmy Tessio. He had a gym of his own and was managing boxers ever since he got discharged from the navy. He used to train fighters to compete in the armed forces championships. Tymes worked out for Tessio, and Tessio liked him enough to take a chance on him.

"Duggett paid up your gym fees for six months. You should be ready to start earning some dough by then. You got to stay clean. No dope, no beer, no weed, nothing. You are getting one chance with me. You mess it up and we are done. Duggett gets no refund. That's it. Understood?"

Tymes shook the small man's hand. "You won't regret it, sir," he answered. Tesio looked at Duggett and smiled. "Thanks for bringing the kid to me. He just might make it. He's good," Tessio said. Turning to Tymes, Tessio told him to show up at his gym tomorrow morning, around nine o'clock. Tymes agreed and climbed into Duggett's car.

Duggett drove them onto the westbound freeway. They merged into the carpool lane and drove past the many open-air swap meets that lined the freeway. The Los Angeles of his childhood memories had morphed into a facade of glitz and glamor that was made for TV but fell short in terms of reality. The disparity of wealth and opportunity was as obvious as the smog that hovered over the valley.

Duggett drove to Los Angeles International Airport, to the departing flights curb. He stopped the Cadillac and popped open the trunk and grabbed a small suitcase.

"Hey, man, where do you think you going?" Tymes laughed.

Duggett handed him the keys to the Seville. "The title is in the glove box. Trigger signed it, but I never did. So just sign your name and register the car in your name." Duggett peeled off five twenties and handed them to Tymes. "Tessio will have some odd jobs for you, just to keep some money in your pocket until you start fighting. Come on out and holler at me when you win the belt."

Tymes took the money and the car keys and shoved them in his pocket. Looking a bit confused, he smiled at Duggett and asked him, "Where the hell are you going, man?"

Duggett shook his hand and then gave him a big hug. "I'm going to P I, baby. The Philippines."

The End

Beast Mode

Det. Judy Garcia pulled her white Range Rover to the curb of the crime scene. It was in a rural area of Fontana, and a couple of uniformed cops were on the scene with yellow tape going across the front door of the victim's house. Garcia was forty-nine years old and had nearly twenty-five years of law enforcement service in Southern California, mainly centered in the Inland Empire. She was due to retire in six months and was dutifully counting the days.

Garcia usually worked homicide cases by herself, but this morning she picked up a brand-new detective from her home in nearby Rancho Cucamonga. Det. Aliya Pezant was thirty years old, an African American, and had earned her master's degree from UCLA and was a rising star in the police department. She made detective after only six years as a uniformed officer.

Garcia parked and pointed to a policeman. "Let's see what they got." The lead police officer on the scene was named Gerald Montoya. He didn't enjoy waiting for detectives to take over the crime scene because they usually arrived late, drinking coffee and eating donuts; rude; condescending; and impatient. He expected an overweight, balding white dude who expected Montoya to have completed all the interrogation work by the time he arrived, but instead he was pleasantly surprised to see Garcia's Range Rover with two female detectives inside pull up.

A second policeman sat in a black and white police cruiser, drinking coffee and chatting on his cell phone. Officer Montoya approached the detectives, said good morning, and then gave them the information he had gathered so far.

"The victim is a sixty-six-year-old white male, ex-con, mostly drug trafficking, some disorderly conduct stuff. Not well liked by any of the neighbors, especially Mr. McMann over there." Montoya motioned across the street, where an elderly black man patiently stood. "I asked him to chat with you when you arrived. He's been waiting about fifteen minutes. He's eager to help. He may be the last person to see Bradley Spooner alive. Spooner is the victim, still lying in bed."

"Why were you guys here doing a welfare check?" Detective Pezant asked.

Montoya cleared his throat and answered with a little more bass in his voice, sounding official and charming at the same time. The older and thicker Garcia smiled. "Well, we got an anonymous call from a friend of his that he was not answering the door. It was probably one of his customers trying to find out if they need a new connection. You can see into the house through the open curtains in the living room window.

Further down the hallway, you can see a corner of the bedroom. Someone is lying on the bed. We obtained a warrant to gain entry and perform a check of the premises. We reported the body inside then we waited for you."

Garcia nodded and looked over at Pezant. She nodded as well. The policeman excused himself. They both waved for the older man to join them. They all said their morning greetings, and then Mr. McMann let go of all the animosity that he had for Spooner.

"If you look up 'asshole' in the dictionary, there would be a picture of Spooner. There's only a few of us neighbors on this road, and he hated all of us, especially me, seeing how I live across from him. I go out to put my trash cans out, and if he be out there too, he shouts at me, 'Good evening, Soul Train.' Then he would give me the finger. I shout right back, 'Good evening, Duck Dynasty!' And I give him the finger right back."

Garcia and Pezant both laughed, and Pezant pointed at the trash cans still on the street. "You saw Mr. Spooner last night?"

McMann nodded. "Sure did. And his dog came over to my back door for food early this morning. He won't take care of his own dog. I buy dog food and a dish, and I don't even own a dog. Her name is Maggie. She's a sheagle. An Australian shepherd and beagle mix. She's a smart, easy-tempered, beautiful animal. But he hates all critters. He sits and shoots at animals from his bedroom window. He was even shooting into other neighbors' backyards." The area was not overly developed, like some of the surrounding housing neighborhoods. There was still room for possum, raccoons, and probably deer.

"Did he have many visitors?' Garcia asked.

"Everyone knew he was dealing drugs, weed, pills, and who knows what else. Lots of traffic, but no one hung out. Nobody liked him," McMann said.

The detectives thanked the man for his help in establishing a timeline and said they would knock on his door if they needed more information. When they entered Spooner's house, they could see that he wasn't much for tidiness. Beer cans, paper trash, and cigarette butts littered the floor. Garcia was wearing her Michael Kors loafers and khakis. She noticed that Pezant wore a sharp business suit with jazzy Michael Kors pumps with three-inch heels.

"Watch your step, Soul Train," Garcia joked at Pezant.

When they entered the bedroom, they saw Spooner's body in bed with a gunshot wound to the temple. A .22-caliber rifle was lying on the floor next to the bed.

"He's in bed, looks like he was not expecting company, no signs of forced entry, the entry wound looks like a .22, but look at the angle, it's really low." Pezant had made a real quick analysis of the crime scene, and they were not even in the room for more than a couple of minutes.

Homegirl is going to scare the socks off the good old boys, thought Garcia. Pezant noticed a security system that was hooked up to a laptop sitting on a nightstand. "Let's see if we can pull up the last twelve hours," Garcia told Pezant.

They checked the three cameras' recordings and saw motion on the backyard camera. Just after midnight, video showed a small dog walking in the backyard. It was probably Maggie as it was the size of a beagle. Then a raccoon slowly walked into frame. The two animals walked in the same direction, toward the back door, and then they were no longer on camera. A few minutes passed, then just for a moment, something went flashing through the backyard from the direction of the back door. Garcia replayed it and saw it was the raccoon, running back into the thick bushes at the edge of the yard.

Garcia walked back to the kitchen that led to the backyard. She saw that Spooner had a doggy door installed on his rear door. It wasn't very large, just big enough for a beagle…or a raccoon to fit through. The dirty mess in the kitchen was worse than the rest of the house, she thought. Looking through the window that sat above the kitchen sink, Garcia spotted a raccoon sitting on the edge of the backyard. Was it the same raccoon as on the laptop? Who could tell?

When Garcia returned to the bedroom, Pezant was inspecting Spooner's head. "There are powder burns on his flesh. The muzzle of the rifle was right up against his head. And if you check the wooden forestock of the rifle, there are teeth marks in the wood. And the shooter had to lie on their belly, on the floor, to get the entry wound at this angle."

Neither woman spoke for close to a minute. Finally, Garcia walked over to the laptop and closed the screen. "Self-inflicted gunshot. Suicide." Garcia stared at Pezant.

Pezant stared back. "Those teeth marks are not human." Pezant pointed at the rifle. "He couldn't reach the trigger if the barrel was against his head," she added.

Garcia looked at the ceiling and then quickly back at Detective Pezant's attractive face. "Baby girl, they don't want us to shine brighter than them. It's been a boys' club for years, and they don't like checking their language and attitudes just because we are in the room. If you file a report, that a dog and raccoon are the likely suspects in a homicide investigation, your career is finished. At the very best, your tenure will end up like mine. And you deserve better than that. They almost made me quit. Now what really happened is Spooner knocked the rifle onto the floor, and it accidentally discharged. The dog picked up the rifle after the shooting, explaining the teeth marks. That's an easy closure."

Pezant was still not buying it. Finally, Garcia grasped Pezant's shoulders. "Do you know why I work alone? Did they tell you?" Pezant nodded that she knew.

The joint operation happened fourteen years ago, before Garcia made detective. A biker gang had set up a big meth lab in an abandoned warehouse in Colton. The DEA had ten agents and ten uniform cops to raid the place. Garcia was one of the officers. DEA placed a Winnebago in Rialto to act as the command center. They could communicate with every officer and monitor a gas detecting device given to each person going inside the warehouse. The device would emit a loud alarm on the device and back at the command center as well if any hazardous gas was nearby. The name of the person wearing the device would also show on the monitor at the command center.

Going inside the warehouse, it appeared the place was deserted. The cooking equipment was still there, but the bikers must have gotten a last-minute tip. Suddenly, Garcia's detector started alarming loudly, and the call over the radio was to evacuate the building immediately. Everyone massed outside to see what happened. After a minute or two, the DEA agent in charge announced over the radio that Garcia's detector took a hit for methane gas. Garcia wore her detector on her service belt; the other agents wore theirs on the collar of the vest. Now she knew why. She had let out a "silent but deadly" fart, and it triggered her detector.

The group of officers and agents erupted with laughter. Humiliated, Garcia handed over her vest and detector and went home. When she returned to the precinct after the weekend, there was a box of odor eaters in her patrol car. Fake police reports were assigned to her, like a burglary at Taco Bell, where someone ate one hundred bean burritos; Officer GAS-cia should sniff out the perps.

Garcia could take a joke as well as anyone, and she even admitted some of the jokes were funny. But things crossed the line one morning in a department meeting when an obese detective named Jefferson slapped her on the rear end and said he could use some gas in his car. She yelled at him to keep his fat, slimy, freewilly hands off her and then proceeded to pummel his face. They both had to go before a discipline hearing. After an internal review, all charges were dropped. An entry into her medical and service record stated that because of severe flatulence, Officer Garcia was not required to share a vehicle or work directly with any other officer. It was a miracle that she made detective.

Pezant could only imagine what Garcia had to endure. "Hey, have you been called Dick-less Tracy?" she asked Garcia. "The men called me that when I graduated first in my class."

Garcia laughed. "I've been called that too. "After the fart incident, they called me Tooty Judy. You file this report as a homicide and the suspect are animals, they are going to say you been transferred to Animal Planet." Garcia let out a big hearty laugh. "And they will send you video of an attempted murder, and it will be a cartoon of the coyote trying to kill the roadrunner." The two detectives howled with laughter.

"Yeah, I guess its silly that a raccoon is going around busting a cap on trailer park drug dealers." She laughed.

Garcia smiled at her. "And with Maggie, the sidekick? The rifle fell off the bed and went off. Case closed."

Pezant nodded. Both women laughed and started to leave the house. Mr. McMann was waiting by Garcia's car with a small dog. "I don't want to call animal control. Maybe you know someone who wants a good dog? I'm allergic, or I would keep Maggie," he said.

Garcia opened the rear door and allowed Maggie to jump inside. "I'll do some asking around," she promised him. As she started the car, Garcia glanced over at Pezant. "You want a dog?" she asked.

"Are you asking me if I want a murderer dog?" Pezant replied.

Garcia laughed. "C'mon, we know this beautiful dog is not a murderer. Besides, the raccoon had to pull the trigger."

Pezant laughed and punched Garcia on the shoulder. "Yeah, why don't you radio in an APB on a murder suspect, two feet tall, weighs twenty-five pounds, wearing a black mask, likes to eat birds' eggs and rotten fruit from garbage cans?" They both laughed.

"Seriously, you should consider keeping the dog, at least for a while. See if you two form a bond together. She seems sweet," Garcia said.

Pezant looked in the back seat at Maggie. She was wagging her tail and appeared to be very happy. She really was a pretty dog. Pezant turned back around in her seat, paused for a second, then declared to Garcia, "OK, let's file the report accidental discharge, possible suicide, call the ambulance to pick up the body, and I will think about what I will do with Maggie here."

Garcia put the car in gear and pulled out into the street. She glanced in her rear-view mirror and noticed Maggie was overly excited and looking out the rear passenger window. Standing at the side of the house was a raccoon. Was it waving? Garcia and the raccoon locked eyes for a second. Garcia was astonished and not sure what she just saw. Hold up. Did that raccoon just give me the finger?

The End

Shadows of Misty Yesteryears

The twin engine Cessna sputtered as it dipped its left wing, circled back over the blue Caribbean Sea, then glided silently like a seagull when the engines finally died. The flight path from southern Florida to Nassau, Bahamas was meticulously checked against other public records to ensure that there would be no shipping vessels or aircraft in this patch of the ocean to assist the survivors of the crash at precisely six thirty P.M. The pilot of the Cessna, Richard Fuentes, radioed the Coast Guard

Joint Rescue Coordination Center that due to engine failure, he was about to ditch the plane into the ocean, along with his employer, Mr. Leon, who was seated next to him. Fuentes controlled the plane as it descended lower towards the water. He was in excellent physical shape and was a former Navy seal and remained calm, keeping the nose of the plane raised for a smoother crash landing. He looked over at Mr. Leon, who was admiring the setting sun resembling an orange globe sinking into the simmering horizon. The sunsets were amazing at this precise- time. That's why he selected this exact time and place to die. Leon appeared to be in his eighties and in good spirits, considering his present situation. Preparing for a wet landing, Fuentes has removed his shoes and taken off his jacket. He offered a portable air bottle with a breathing mask to Mr. Leon, who shook his head no and pointed to the small vial that Fuentes kept in his shirt pocket. Laughing, Fuentes handed over his small vial of coke. "I'm keeping this, selfish son of a bitch," Leon smirked.

"Of course, sir. How thoughtless of me," Fuentes replied, admiring the older mans' sense of humor while facing imminent death. The old man quickly took a hit in each nostril and smiled at the younger man.

"Be careful, son. Of the world, I mean." Fuentes gave the signal to brace for impact and grasped the old mans' hand. Crashing into the ocean, the small plane mostly disintegrated, both wings cartwheeling across the oceans' surface. The cabin quickly filled with seawater as Fuentes loosened his seat belt and began to crawl out the open space where the window used to be. Fuentes waited a few seconds to let the plane fully submerge beneath the waves, then planted his feet to launch himself back to the surface. One last look at his beloved employer, Mr. Leon, was a sight to behold. The old man remained in his seat belt, a huge grin on his face after taking another snort of coke and flipping Fuentes the double bird. Fuentes nearly gulped water into his lungs trying his best not to laugh out-loud.

He saluted his boss and swam to the surface to await a rescue team.

Ten days later, a memorial service was held for Patrick de Leon, owner of Leon beauty products, at the manufacturing site and home office in Clearwater, Florida. His given age was listed at eighty-seven years old. His chief financial officer, Carlos Madura, was slated to take over the day-to-day operations, which most people felt he was doing for years anyway. The gathering was limited to only a few important people in the beauty product industry and politicians, and a few local reporters. Mr. Leon left no living relatives and his remaining assets were to be distributed among various charities. A local catering services, Kissimmee Katerers, had been hired to serve food and drinks for the gathering and they also handled the valet parking services. Carlos Madura looked to be about fifty-five years old, slightly greying at the temples, and in good physical shape. Most of the employees of Leon Products appeared to be in excellent health. Carlos stood next to a large photograph of Patrick de Leon and spoke to guests as they conveyed their condolences to the friends and associates of Mr. Leon. His head of security, Glen Harden, a former army ranger and CIA analyst, walked close to Carlos to whisper a message.

"We got a hit on the serving staff," Harden says. Madura nods.

Time passed slowly for Kate Tranton. She was on the serving line for three hours and was about to unplug the electric food warming stations, as the last guests had left the service. The other employees of the catering service were also breaking down their stations. Her name tag identified her as Jenny Watson and she had to explain to her coworkers that she was a last minute replacement for the real Jenny, who abruptly quit and left her uniform and name tag at the office without further explanation. Kate was using her uniform and ID tag because there was no time for her to get her own stuff issued to her. Her coworkers bought the fabricated lie because they really didn't care. Glen Harden was a different story altogether. He approached Kate/Jenny and held her arm gently, yet firm.

"Let your friends clean up. Mr. Madura would like to have a word with you in his office," he told her. She looked up at the large man.

"It seems as I don't have a choice," she says.

"That's right. This way, please," Harden answered. Harden used his ID badge to unlock a door which opened to a long hallway. They walked in silence, except for the sound of their heels clicking on the polished marble floor. For a company that made beauty products, the level of security was extremely exorbitant, on par with any bank or casino that she knew of. From her apartment in Washington D.C., she tried, unsuccessfully, to hack into the mainframe of Leon enterprises, but was stopped at the digital firewall by a cartoon grandma that appeared on her laptop screen, wagging her finger and saying "Shame on you trying to enter my house uninvited. How do you sleep in your car at night?" Kates' obsession with Leon enterprises had nothing to do with criminal undertaking or any illicit activity. Just the opposite was true. The company annually makes several notable contributions to charities and foundations. Recently, Leon donated millions of dollars-worth of their top selling nourishing treatments to several hospital burn centers. As an investigating reporter for the Post, Kate smelled that something wasn't kosher with Leon enterprises and she also smelled a big story. Kates' original plan was to slip away from the caterers to scout out the manufacturing area. Her interest was in building forty-three in the manufacturing chemical process. The architectural engineering drawings that were submitted to the city for approval during construction, identified this building as the water processing area. Ordinarily, this building is where imported mud from the Dead Sea in Jordan or the Nile River in Egypt would be saturated with water and other essential nutrients, but the drawings showed no evidence of water supply piping entering the building. So, where did the water come from? It was possible that there was an above ground water supply, however it would still have to be documented on the drawings, which were official public records. She just planned on doing a quick visual check and claim to be on a smoke break if she was stopped by security. A background check on several members of the security department revealed that most of the employees had prior military experience, including special forces training. Finally releasing Kates' arm, Harden shoves her inside a large office with a beamed ceiling and several museum pieces and artifacts decorating it in a worldly style. Carlos Madura sat behind a large mahogany desk and motioned for her to come and sit at one of the two cushioned chairs that were in front of his desk. His chair had a high back and was upholstered in deep red leather.

"Please have a seat, Kate. You worked very long tonight. I'm sure you must be tired." Kate walked over and sat down a little hesitantly and Harden motioned to Carlos that he would be outside if needed.

"How do you know who I am and why did you allow me to work all night if you knew I wasn't the real Jenny?" she asked. Carlos pointed at several cameras in his office.

"We have cameras everywhere and facial recognition software. You were doing well with your tip jar. I let you make some cash. Don't they pay you well at the Washington Post? Is this a moonlighting gig for you? To travel to Florida from Washington, I would think your expenses are too big to be covered by your tips, eh?" Kate was surprised that he knew she was an investigative reporter for the Washington Post newspaper. She graduated from Georgetown University with a degree in chemistry and continued to get her masters at Harvard. She worked for the Food and Drug Administration for ten years before moving on to journalism, which was her real passion. She was thirty-eight years old with shoulder length, auburn hair. She has been divorced for the last three years, largely because she had been so dedicated to her work at the Post, she hardly noticed or cared about how much time her husband was spending with his attractive assistant. He asked for a divorce and she complied. "So where is the real Jenny Watson? Did you bump her off?" Carlos teased.

"I gave her two hundred bucks to stay home and loan me her uniform," Kate answered. Carlos Madura leaned forward on his desk to speak to Kate.

"You are aware that we offer a guided tour of our processing plant every Wednesday? Of course, you know this because you have taken the tour twice before and our facial recognition matched you tonight impersonating Jenny Watson. The million-dollar question remains unanswered; why? Why have you come to our facility to spy on us during the memorial service of our esteemed founder? A formal request for an interview would have been much more professional, don't you agree?" Kate leaned forward over the mahogany desk; meeting Carlos nearly nose to nose.

"I did request an interview. Ten times. Each time I was told that you don't do interviews. However, Mr. Madura, you did do one interview. At the St. Louis worlds' fair. In St. Louis, Missouri. In St. Louis, Missouri in 1904." Kate leaned back into her chair and tried to read Carlos' reaction. It seemed as if the eyes in his head just became a darker shade of black. His gaze went right through her as if he was looking back into the past.

"I killed two men who tried to rob me at that fair," he whispered. Carlos was not a large man. He was not of Latin descent, like Mr. Leon, he was native. Kate felt the temperature in the room drop a few degrees and she became frightened. Carlos Madura looked like he was in a trance, sitting motionless, the eyes were a deep dark void, empathy and compassion had abruptly abandoned his soul. Kate scanned the room for a potential weapon to defend herself when Carlos Madura slowly started to smile. He clapped his hands together. "I knew it. It was only a matter of time that you would discover something unusual was afoot. You are persistent and tenacious. We have monitored you routinely ever since you have taken an overzealous interest in our business. Tell me all that has piqued your interest in us." Kate sighed and unclenched her grip on the wooden arms of her chair.

"Well, I became curious about the pH levels in the water composition of your product while I worked at FDA. There were very inconsistent readings. Sometimes the levels were high and sometimes the levels were low." Carlos raised his finger to make a point.

"Yes, that's because our water reacts differently for each customer. It seeks the correct balance and adjusts to that level." Now, Kate raised both hands for a pause.

"That's not how the chemistry in water works. The pH balance of $H2O$ is a standard for all chemical measurements," she says. Carlos laughs and shakes his head.

"Our process water causes a slightly different reaction. It's really very simple to understand. I can show you how we do it." If Kate was afraid earlier, now she was terrified. Why was Madura sharing details that have been kept hidden as a closely guarded enigma? She wondered if she was going to be allowed to leave intact.

"You should know that I have people that are aware that I am here. If something should happen to me, it will be investigated," she told Carlos. He shook his head and winced as if wounded.

"I can assure you that there is no reason for concern," he replied. Carlos stood up from behind the desk and walked to a wall cabinet and retrieved a small bottled water. He was less than average in height but very stocky. "Kate, you should know that every time you looked at us, we looked back at you. We know your editor at the Post sent you here on a fact-finding mission because you assured him that you would have a story worthy of the front page. He was not convinced, but he sent you anyway because of your reputation as a hard worker. Of course, he knows you are here. Your mother in Silver Spring, Maryland; your sister in Hampton, Virginia; your ex-husband in Dupont Circle, Washington D.C.; and possibly your nephew attending school in Bloomington, Indiana. They may also know that you are here. And we know where they are, as well. When you breached our security, our automatic response is to dispatch contractors to your most prized assets. If you attack us, we hurt you back. Tenfold. Your ex-husband may not carry much weight, but he is in our records of people close to you. I give you my word that no harm will befall you or anyone associated with you," he said. Now Kate stood up and stood face to face with Carlos.

"Let me thank you for not; what was the word you used? Oh yeah, bumping off my family. What a great humanitarian you are," she sarcastically noted. Carlos reached for another bottled water and handed it to her. She twisted off the cap took a short swallow. "And can you explain how you can attend the state fair at the turn of the century, making you over one hundred years old? I mean, I'm trying to understand just what the hell kind of beauty products company are you? Are you a front for the CIA? Your security is way over the top," she said. Carlos chuckled and sipped his water.

"No way are we affiliated with the CIA or any government agency. Our security is here to protect our trade secrets and out intellectual property. I can give you a tour of our site, including the water processing building, and I think everything will become clearer. And one hundred years is a very modest estimate concerning my age. I guess I should thank you for the compliment. Come with me, please," he said, walking to the door. Glen Harden, the security guy, escorted Carlos and Kate outside to an electric golf cart parked by the side of the building.

"Hunky Dory?" Harden asked Carlos as he sat inside the cart, preparing to drive.

"Copacetic," Carlos replied. Kate looked at Carlos for an explanation of the obviously coded exchange between the two men. "The contractors are being recalled from your family's homes," he told her. While riding in the golf cart, Kate told Carlos about the missing water pipes at building forty-three and he made a mental note to add above ground water pipes to supply restrooms, air conditioning, and even an indoor koi pond. She asked him why he didn't command a larger salary, as Leon products were far superior to the other brands and his company supplies most of the high-end resorts and spas. Even the reasonably priced factory seconds, sold in discount stores, are bought out immediately. "We have invested a lot of money into research and development in several areas of experimentation, not only beauty products. We use our process water for irrigation on different crops and then donate the food we grow to schools, orphanages, and refugee centers. We discovered the healing effects of using our water to counter dementia and Alzheimer's disease, the improvements are modest, yet very successful. We package IV kits and sell them, at just a little above cost, to VA hospitals and assisted living centers. Kate, I assure you that we are not a bunch of mad scientists attempting to take over the world." Questions still swirled in her head despite the enlightening information from Carlos.

"I have dug up nothing but positive things in my research of your company. Your humanitarian donations are most admirable, but when something seems too good to be true, it usually is. For instance, in your interview, over one hundred years ago, you mentioned that you were from the Calusa Indian tribe. They have been extinct for over three hundred years. But here you are, alive and well, driving a golf cart like the Last of the Mohicans." Carlos laughed loudly and smacked the steering wheel.

"You know something, I told the Spaniards that I am Calusa. They thought I was saying that my name is Carlos. I just went with it. What the hell. Why not?" Carlos parked the cart near the front door of the water processing building. At the front door, Carlos scanned his ID badge and placed his thumb on a scanner door lock. The door beeped, unlocked, and he pulled the door open for Kate to enter. The overhead lights came on, activated by motion detectors. The inside of the building looked like a large warehouse with a loading dock and forklift in the rear of the building. A roll up door led out to the loading dock and just off to the side was a separate room with another locked door. After unlocking the door, the two of them walk about ten feet and see a small pool in the center of the room. It stretched out about four feet wide and six feet deep and only half filled with water. "That's the key to our success, Kate," Carlos said. Kate looked puzzled.

"I don't get it," she tells him.

"Yes, I know it's not very impressive to look at, but it is a gift from heaven, nonetheless. That is the legendary fountain of youth," he tells her. He finds a folding chair stacked against the wall and brings it over to her. She sits down on the chair with a deep sigh.

"So, the deceased owner, Mr. Leon, was a descendant of Ponce de Leon?" Carlos stood before her with the widest grin on his face. Then she understood just what he was implying. "NO WAY!" she shouted. Carlos handed her another bottled water from a shelf on the wall.

"The plane crash was planned. He was tired of continuing to just exist when he felt he had seen enough. He chose to go down into the sea. We tampered with the fuel line to make it look like an accident and our pilot, Richard Fuentes, is an excellent swimmer. A funny story is that Fuentes and my security officer, Harden, were on opposite sides of the battle at the Alamo. There was at least one survivor at the Alamo," Carlos told her. She gulped down half of her bottled water.

"Everyone here at this company is immortal?" she asked.

"No, there are only twenty of us left that are privileged with the secret. There were more, but many have had accidents or got careless or just got tired of living. The water does not grant immunity to disease or bullets. It merely slows down the aging process and has some rejuvenation qualities. If you stop drinking the water, then father time plays a catch-up game and your true age will eventually begin to show, keeping our repeat sales incredibly high and maintaining a high level of customer loyalty. The water you have been drinking today is not for retail purposes. It's not as diluted as what we offer to the public consumer. It's what we drink daily. How do you feel, Kate?" She took a deep breath and exhaled slowly. It only took a moment for her to realize the difference in her posture and physical well-being. She felt great. She felt zestful and energetic. The nagging pain in her lower back that she had learned to live with since her car accident years ago, had mostly disappeared.

"Why not share this miracle with the whole medical community and with government assets to different distribution centers so many more people can benefit?" she asked him.

"Kate, the Spaniards used the water to prolong the health of the slave workforce of the captive Indians. The highest-ranking officer, Santiago, was cruel and sadistic and often tortured the natives to test the recuperating powers of the water. He took pleasure in causing pain and inflicting injuries. His soul became corrupted by absolute power and turned him into a living, evil, deitylike being. Ponce de Leon, along with like-minded soldiers, led a revolt by the Indians and killed Santiago and his staff. Kate, men have not changed much in the last several hundred years. Captains of industries, influential politicians, financial institutions are not unlike mafia organizations in their quest for more. Big pharmaceutical companies and insurance firms would create a monopoly and control who gets treated and who doesn't, largely dependent on the ability to pay hefty fees. The charitable contributions and donations would end immediately. There would be lawsuits, deceit, and murder among all the controlling factions. But, most importantly, the source is slowly drying up. It evens stops flowing from time to time, then resumes flowing again, with a slightly lower flow rate. We don't know why it stops or for how much longer it will last. "He paused and sipped his water. "The pool is lined with C4 explosives. Enough to destroy the fountain ten times over. We will control and protect the water with our lives, if needed, and never allow another like Santiago to exploit it. We have bought off, scared off, and killed the ones to stubborn to leave us alone. I will completely destroy it before I let immoral criminals in expensive suits make deplorable profits from this gift." Kate stood up from her chair and knelt beside the pool.

"Why are you telling me these things that you have kept hidden from the world for so long?" Carlos placed his hand on her shoulder, gently.

"I'm hoping that you join us. All the time you were looking at us, I was watching you also, thinking how perfect you would fit in, if you believed in our cause." Kate stood up and looked closely at the crows' feet around Carlos' eyes.

"Did you ever consider just asking me if I would be interested?"

"You can never catch a butterfly by chasing it, you wait until it lands upon your shoulder. Trust is earned," he replied. The pair stood silently and listened to the slow trickle of water churning into the pool. "

Now what?" she asked. He walked and held the door open for her.

"Now you return to Washington. You will either write a nice, flowery piece about my company, which will infuriate your editor. Or you will disclose all that you learned down here, and I will await my fate. Our new hire indoctrination class begins in a couple of weeks, in the event of the editor of the Washington Post fires you, you are most welcome here." She left the facilities and caught an Uber to her hotel, grabbed a sandwich from a machine, watched Netflix for an hour and went to bed. The next morning on her flight back to D.C., she composed her notes for the article she would submit. Two weeks later, the Leon beauty products corporate newsletter proudly announced that

Kate Tranton has joined the company as the manager of Public Relations at the headquarter and manufacturing facility in Clearwater, Florida. Kate laid the newsletter upon her mahogany desk and looked out of her window at the breathtaking rose garden Carlos added outside her office. Her office was exactly twenty square feet larger than his. She locked her fingers together behind her head and leaned backwards in her chair with a high back and upholstered in deep red leather. "It may take a little time, but I think I can get used to this," she thought to herself.

The End